mini ENCYCLOPEDIA

SPACE

Contents

The Universe	4
Galaxies	6
Stars	8
The Solar System	10
The Sun	12
The Earth and Moon	14
Mercury, Venus, and Mars	16
Jupiter	18
Saturn	20
Uranus and Neptune	22
Space exploration	24
Satellites	26
The International Space Station	28
Glossary	30
Index	31

The Universe

The Earth is just a tiny part of the enormous Universe. We do not know how big the Universe actually is, but we know that it is bigger than we can ever imagine.

How far away?

When we look at the stars and the Sun, they look small. Our Sun is actually a million times bigger than the Earth, but it is also over 90 million miles (150 million km) away, which is why it looks small to us.

Some scientists believe that the Universe was created in an enormous explosion called the Big Bang over 13 billion years ago. Ever since the Universe began, it has been growing. Scientists think that it may keep growing forever.

Gravity

If you throw a ball in the air, it will always come down. The force that pulls the ball down towards the ground is called gravity. Without gravity, things like the air and people would all float off into space. It is also gravity that keeps the Earth and the other planets circling around the Sun, and the Moon circling around the Earth.

Galaxies

Our entire Solar System is part of a galaxy called the Milky Way. A galaxy is a huge structure made up of billions of stars, dust, and gas, which are all held together by gravity. The Sun is just one of the stars in the Milky Way!

Galaxies can form in different shapes. The Milky Way is called a barred spiral galaxy.

Types of galaxy

Irregular galaxy: a galaxy without a regular shape

Spiral galaxy: a bright center with two or more arms spiraling out

Elliptical galaxy: round or oval shaped galaxies

6

There is a bright bar of stars in the center and several curved arms spiraling out.

Galaxies also collect together into groups called clusters.

Sun

Our Solar System is here.

Seeing the Milky Way

You may be able to see the Milky Way on a clear night. It looks like a misty band stretched across the sky.

Cartwheel Galaxy: a galaxy that may have been shaped by a crash with a smaller galaxy

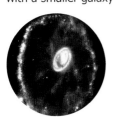

The Milky Way at night

Stars

Stars fill our night sky. A star is a huge ball of hot gas that is held together by gravity. Even though the stars are very far away, we can see them shining in the dark because they give out a lot of light.

Some stars look bright because they are close to Earth. Other bright stars are giant stars that give out a lot of light.

Shooting stars

Shooting stars are flashes of light that fly across the sky. They are actually small pieces of ice and rock called meteors, which get very hot and glow brightly when they enter the Earth's atmosphere. A piece of meteor that manages to pass through a planet's atmosphere and reach the ground is called a meteorite.

Constellations

Some groups of stars seem to make patterns in the sky. These patterns are called constellations. We use our imagination to see people and animals in the shapes of the constellations.

The Big Dipper, part of The Great Bear

Stars are different colors depending on how hot they are. Red stars are cool and blue stars are very hot.

Stars can live for millions of years. The Sun is a small star in the middle of its life. It will keep on giving heat and light for another five thousand million years!

The Solar System

Our Solar System includes the Sun, eight planets, moons, asteroids, comets, and dust. The Sun, the planets, and moons all spin around. The planets are all held in circular paths around the Sun by the Sun's gravity. These circular paths are called orbits.

Neptune

Pluto

Pluto is now called a dwarf planet. Scientists have discovered several other dwarf planets like Pluto, which are all a long way from the Sun.

A planet's day is the time it takes to spin all the way around. The Earth's day lasts for 24 hours.

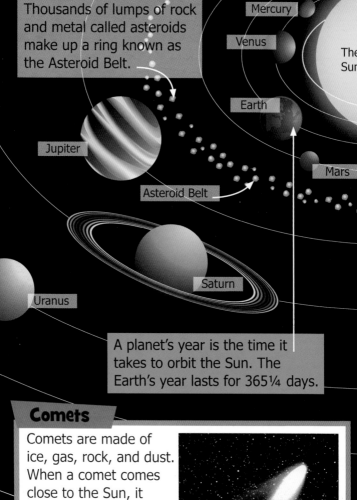

Thousands of lumps of rock and metal called asteroids make up a ring known as the Asteroid Belt.

Mercury

Venus

The Sun

Earth

Jupiter

Asteroid Belt

Mars

Saturn

Uranus

A planet's year is the time it takes to orbit the Sun. The Earth's year lasts for 365¼ days.

Comets

Comets are made of ice, gas, rock, and dust. When a comet comes close to the Sun, it warms up and leaves a trail of gas and dust behind. We call this trail a comet's tail.

The Sun

Without the Sun, there would be no heat or light and therefore no life on Earth. The Sun is in the middle of our Solar System, and like all stars, it is a big ball of extremely hot gas. The other planets and moons are held in their orbits around the Sun by the Sun's gravity.

Solar eclipse

When the Moon passes between the Earth and the Sun, it can completely block out the Sun's light. This is called a solar eclipse. A solar eclipse is the only time that we can see the white haze of gases that surround the Sun.

Solar flares are explosions of gas on the Sun's surface.

The core is at the center of the Sun. It is the hottest part.

Sunspots look like dark patches on the Sun's surface. They are slightly cooler than the rest of the surface.

You should never look directly at the Sun. It is very bad for your eyes and could blind you.

The Earth and Moon

The Earth is our home planet. It is made of rock and is the third planet from the Sun. The Earth is the only planet in our Solar System that can support life, as far as we know. The Moon orbits the Earth. It is the Sun's light upon the Moon that makes it shine.

Changing Moon

Each month, the Moon seems to change shape. As the Moon orbits the Earth, the Sun lights up more and more of the Moon, until it appears as a full Moon. The Moon takes about 27 days to complete one orbit around the Earth.

Moon phases

New Moon

Crescent

Half Moon

14

The Moon's surface is covered with holes or craters, caused by collisions with meteorites.

Surrounding the Earth is a blanket of air called the atmosphere. It protects us from some of the Sun's harmful rays and gives us varied weather.

Oceans cover more of the Earth's surface than land.

Unlike the other planets, the Earth's surface is not solid, but is split up into pieces called plates.

Full Moon

Half Moon

Decrescent

Mercury, Venus, and Mars

The other rocky planets in our Solar System are Mercury, Venus, and Mars. Mercury is the smallest planet and is closest to the Sun, but it is Venus that is the hottest of all the planets. Mars is a cold, rocky planet, with temperatures usually below freezing.

Mercury

Mercury is covered in craters.

It takes Mercury just 88 days to orbit the Sun.

Mars is called the Red Planet because it is covered in red dust.

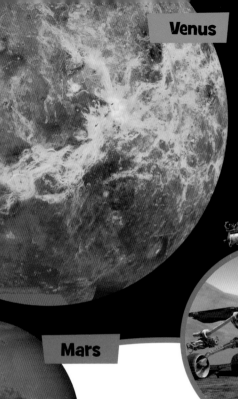

You can see Venus shining in our night sky for most of the year. It is a similar size to Earth, but it has many volcanoes covering its surface and thick clouds made of acid.

Mars

Mars has two moons called Phobos, which means fear, and Deimos, which means terror!

Exploring Mars

There have been many missions to explore Mars. In 2004, two robots called Spirit and Opportunity landed on the surface of Mars. They have sent back many full-color images of the planet.

Jupiter

Jupiter is the giant planet of our Solar System. It is mostly made of gases and liquids, but even its rocky core is as much as twenty times the size of the Earth.

Spots show the tremendous thunderstorms that take place where the clouds in Jupiter's atmosphere meet.

Io is one of Jupiter's moons. It has many active volcanoes.

The Great Red Spot is a raging storm of swirling clouds that has existed for over 300 years. It is so large that the Earth could fit inside it three times!

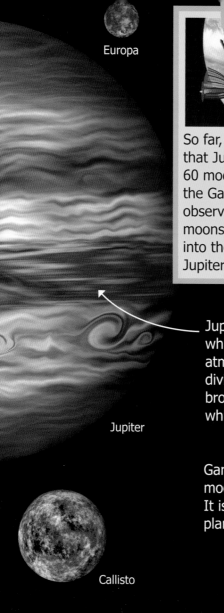

Europa

So far, we have discovered that Jupiter has more than 60 moons. For eight years, the Galileo space probe observed Jupiter and its moons, before plunging into the atmosphere of Jupiter in 2003.

Jupiter spins quickly, which causes its atmosphere to divide into bands of brown, orange, and white clouds.

Jupiter

Ganymede is the largest moon in our Solar System. It is even larger than the planet Mercury.

Callisto

Saturn

Famous for its impressive rings, Saturn is the sixth planet from the Sun. Like Jupiter, Saturn is a giant gas planet, but if you could find an ocean large enough, it would be light enough to float in water! In 2004, the Cassini spacecraft reached Saturn. It has been helping us to explore the planet.

Saturn

Light and dark

So far, we have discovered more than 60 moons orbiting Saturn. Titan is Saturn's largest moon. Iapetus is another of Saturn's moons. Half of Iapetus is as white as snow, while half is dark black.

Like Jupiter, Saturn has a rocky core and bands of clouds on its surface.

There is gap between two of Saturn's rings. This is called the Cassini Division.

Saturn's rings are thick enough to create a shadow on the planet.

Saturn's ice rings

Some pieces of ice in Saturn's rings are as small as sand grains, while others are as large as cars! Saturn's rings are made up of billions of pieces of ice. They may be fragments of a moon that smashed to pieces in a collision millions of years ago.

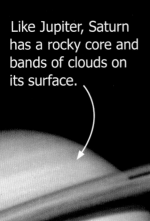
Saturn's rings

Uranus and Neptune

Billions of miles away from the Sun are the final two gas giants in our Solar System: the icy planets, Uranus and Neptune. Most of the information we know about these distant planets has come from the space probe, Voyager 2, which flew past them in the 1980s.

Although difficult to see, both planets have faint rings surrounding them.

Uranus

Did you know?

Uranus is a blue-green color and Neptune is a bright blue color. This is because of a gas called methane in both planets' atmospheres.

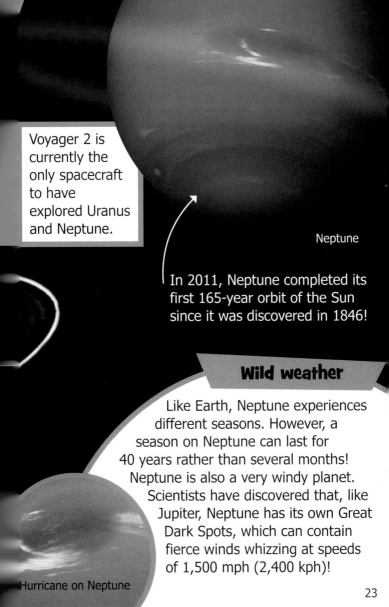

Voyager 2 is currently the only spacecraft to have explored Uranus and Neptune.

Neptune

In 2011, Neptune completed its first 165-year orbit of the Sun since it was discovered in 1846!

Wild weather

Like Earth, Neptune experiences different seasons. However, a season on Neptune can last for 40 years rather than several months! Neptune is also a very windy planet. Scientists have discovered that, like Jupiter, Neptune has its own Great Dark Spots, which can contain fierce winds whizzing at speeds of 1,500 mph (2,400 kph)!

Hurricane on Neptune

Space exploration

People have been studying space for hundreds of years, but it was only in 1609, when Galileo first used a telescope to look at the sky, that we were able to start studying the secrets of the Universe in more detail.

Landing on the moon

In 1969, the Apollo 11 spacecraft landed on the Moon. The three astronauts on the mission were Buzz Aldrin, Neil Armstrong, and Michael Collins. Neil Armstrong and Buzz Aldrin set foot on the Moon. While they were there, they completed experiments, took pictures, and collected moon rocks.

Voyager 1 and 2

Voyager 1 and 2 are machines called space probes that were sent into space in 1977. During their exploration of our Solar System, they have sent back amazing pictures and information.

Keck telescopes

The two powerful Keck telescopes have allowed us to see far into space. They have been built on mountaintops in Hawaii.

Satellites

A satellite is something that travels continuously around a larger object. The natural satellite of our Earth is the Moon, but the Earth also has man-made satellites. These are machines that have been launched into space in order to send and receive signals and to take pictures of the Earth.

How do satellites stay in orbit?

A satellite travels around the Earth on a curved path, or orbit. As it travels, a satellite tries to move in a straight line away from the Earth, while gravity pulls it into a curved path. Provided the speed of the satellite is just right, this curved path forms a complete circle around the Earth and the satellite stays in orbit.

Global positioning satellites (GPS) make it possible to identify exactly where someone or something is on the Earth's surface.

Satellite tries to move away

Gravity

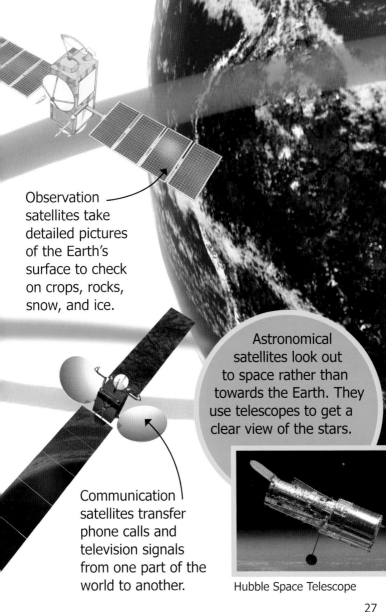

Observation satellites take detailed pictures of the Earth's surface to check on crops, rocks, snow, and ice.

Astronomical satellites look out to space rather than towards the Earth. They use telescopes to get a clear view of the stars.

Communication satellites transfer phone calls and television signals from one part of the world to another.

Hubble Space Telescope

The International Space Station

In 1998, people started work on the International Space Station (ISS) — a spacecraft giving astronauts a place to live and study in outer space. The ISS is now about the size of an American football field, and with the help of other nations, people continue to add to it.

Solar panels use sunlight to create power for the ISS.

The ISS is the largest man-made object to orbit the Earth. You can even see it moving through the sky without a telescope.

Launching into space

Astronauts have traveled into space using rockets and space shuttles. These spacecraft have huge booster rockets that help them to travel very quickly through the air and out of the Earth's atmosphere without being dragged back down to the ground by gravity.

There are laboratories on the ISS for astronauts to do experiments and research.

During one day, the ISS orbits the Earth about 16 times.

Glossary

This glossary explains some of the harder words in the book.

asteroid A lump of rock and metal from outer space that moves around the Sun.

atmosphere The gases that surround the Earth or another planet.

booster The part of a rocket that helps a spacecraft to speed through the air.

comet An object from outer space made of ice, gas, rock, and dust.

core The central part of a planet or star.

crater A large hole made on the surface of a planet or another object.

force A push or pull that can move an object.

gas An air-like substance that can spread out to fill any available space. A gas is not a liquid or a solid.

gravity A force that pulls objects towards each other. On Earth, gravity pulls us towards the ground.

liquid A watery or oil-like substance that flows freely. A liquid substance is not a gas or a solid.

meteor An object made of ice and rock from outer space. It glows brightly on entering the Earth's atmosphere.

mission A job or task given to a group of people. Astronauts complete missions to explore space.

orbit The circular path that something makes around a star or another planet.

planet A large object in outer space that circles around a star. The Earth is a planet that circles around the Sun.

solid Something that has a firm and stable shape. A solid substance is not a liquid or a gas.

spacecraft A vehicle that is used to travel in space.

space probe A machine that is sent to explore space without anybody inside it.

space shuttle A vehicle that is launched by rockets and is used to make journeys between the Earth and space.

telescope An instrument that allows us to make faraway objects appear closer so that we can see them more clearly.